Until De

"The Day that Debt Died"

"Now there cried a certain woman of the wives of the sons of the prophets unto Elisha, saying, Thy servant my husband is dead; and thou knowest that thy servant did fear the LORD: and the creditor is come to take unto him my two sons to be bondmen." 2 Kings 4:1

Apostle Lester Coward

UWriteit Publishing Company
Goldsboro, NC USA
www.uwriteitpublishingcompany.com
"Let us publish your book for you."

ISBN: **ISBN-13: 978-0615651576 (UWriteIt Publishing Company)**
ISBN-10: 0615651577

First Printing June – 2012

Unless otherwise indicated, Scripture quotations in this book are
from the King James Version of the Bible.

This publication is designed to provide information in regard to the
subject matter covered. It is published with the understanding that
the authors are not engaged in rendering legal counsel or other
professional services. If legal advice or other professional advice is
required, the services of a professional person should be sought.

Printed in the U.S.A.

Dedication

I dedicate this book to my secretary Mrs. Annette Harper, a dedicated servant of the Lord.

Table of Contents

Introduction

Introduction

This is the financial book that you've always wanted to have in your possession. Through this book you will discover an abundance of revelation knowledge that will bring a change in your financial life. You don't have to live a life of barely making ends meet, paycheck to paycheck living or a hand to mouth existence. The God of the Bible is able to do exceedingly abundantly above all that you can ask or think according to the power that worketh in you. Ephesians 3:20

If you're ready to see the hand of God in your finances and ready to say bye, bye to debt then hold on to your seat for the ride of your life. Do you want?

- Miracle money
- Supernatural provision
- A Lump Sum
- Amazing occurrence in your finances
- Marvelous and phenomenon events manifesting in your money
- To see debt die
- Wonders that only God can perform

Then get ready to experience the mighty hand of God in your finances as you see the day debt died. Let us behold the scenario; "Debt struggled on for years unwilling to depart from the life of the beholder. But the day came when debt died after many years of struggle. Debt was a tough fight and it held on until the end, but it finally had to say good bye because it's captive finally got the knowledge that could lay it to rest. The funeral procession was preached by none other than Apostle Lester Coward and he preached the gospel and sent debt to hell, its final resting place and forbid it to return to the life of its captive. Now debt has departed and doesn't live there anymore and now prosperity and abundance resides because one man had the tenacity and courage to preach debt back to hell. Get ready to go on a journey of inspiration, motivation and change that will take you from debt to deliverance; here is the dawning of a new day the day that debt died and wealth came alive.

About the Author

Apostle Lester Coward is a native of Kinston, NC. He is the Pastor of Deliverance Temple Revival Center Church Inc. located in Dudley, NC. He started preaching the gospel in 1954 and operates in all the five-fold ministry gifts. He has traveled extensively throughout the east and west coast evangelizing and preaching a prophetic deliverance message that sets the captives free, sets at liberty those that are bruised and binding up the broken heart. He has authored two other books entitled; **"Deliverance At Any Cost and Catching Hell And Calling It A Good Time."** Apostle Coward is an end time preacher with an end time message.

1

Poor No More

"Save when there shall be no poor among you; for the LORD *shall greatly bless thee in the land which the* LORD *thy God giveth thee for an inheritance to possess it: Only if thou carefully hearken unto the voice of the* LORD *thy God, to observe to do all these commandments which I command thee this day." Deuteronomy 15:4-5*

As a Christian God doesn't want you down and out, God wants you to have an abundant life. You were born to be blessed with the best. If you are a child of God you don't have to be poor. The bible says, *"the poor you will have with you always and the poor will never cease." Mark 14:7, Deuteronomy 15:11* But you don't have to be one of the poor. Out of the ashes I rise, God wants to get you out of the ashes. Here are some things about the poor.

- *Wealth maketh many friends; but the poor is separated from his neighbour. Proverbs 19:4*
- *The poor is hated even of his own neighbour: but the rich hath many friends. Proverbs 14:20*

Some people are poor by choice and want to be poor. You got to pull yourself out of that poor mentality. Low and humble is the way but you don't have to stay low. Sometimes you hear people say we were always poor and nobody in our family had anything, well it is time for you to reverse the curse.

You were born to taste the grapes and wine and have some oil. When you get born again you are a royal child, born into royalty, broke no more and poor no more. The struggle is over; your attitude must be **"I am not struggling no more."**

God wants you to have money to do things with. Two broke people and two poor people cannot help each other. You were born to have some money!

Can God Trust You With Your Own Money

There are people that have trouble telling the truth about their own money. In the bible we have the story of Ananias, with Sapphira his wife and it says, *"But a certain man named Ananias, with Sapphira his wife, sold a possession, And kept back part of the price, his wife also being privy to it, and brought a certain part, and laid it at the apostles' feet. But Peter said, Ananias, why hath Satan filled thine heart to lie to the Holy Ghost, and to keep back part of the price of the land? Whiles it remained, was it not thine own? and after it was sold, was it not in thine own power? why hast thou conceived this thing in thine heart? thou hast not lied unto men, but unto God. And Ananias hearing these words fell down, and gave up the ghost: and great fear came on all them that heard these things.*

And the young men arose, wound him up, and carried him out, and buried him. And it was about the space of three hours after, when his wife, not knowing what was done, came in. And Peter answered unto her, Tell me whether ye sold the land for so much? And she said, Yea, for so much.

Then Peter said unto her, How is it that ye have agreed together to tempt the Spirit of the Lord? behold, the feet of them which have buried thy husband are at the door, and shall carry thee out. Then fell she down straightway at his feet, and yielded up the ghost: and the young men came in, and found her dead, and, carrying her forth, buried her by her husband. And great fear came upon all the church, and upon as many as heard these things." Acts 5:1-11

If you will lie about your own money what about your own tithes and offerings?

- **Does money master you or do you master money?**
- **Are you tight handed in giving money for the gospel?**
- **What is the biggest piece of money that you gave in an offering at one time?**

You can only reap what you sow, the scripture says, *"But this I say, He which soweth sparingly shall reap also sparingly; and he which soweth bountifully shall reap also bountifully. Every man according as he purposeth in his heart, so let him give; not grudgingly, or of necessity: for God loveth a cheerful giver. And God is able to make all grace abound toward you; that ye, always having all sufficiency in all things, may abound to every good work."* 2 Corinthians 9:6-8

What Happens When God Blows On Your Money

"Ye have sown much, and bring in little; ye eat, but ye have not enough; ye drink, but ye are not filled with drink; ye clothe you, but there is none warm; and he that earneth wages earneth wages to put it into a bag with holes."
Haggai 1:6

I see and know people that cannot hold on to money or get money. A blow fly will blow on meats or a wound and leave eggs on it and make it unfit. When you rob God of his tithes and offerings he will blow on your money. Some people make big money and don't know where it went, God blew on it. When God blows on your money you will not be able to pay your bills.

People may be trying to help you and give you favour but God can blow on that favour and help and nothing will work for you. You will find yourself in a bind and can't get out. God will blow on what you thought you had and blow so hard on what you had that it will take it all on bills.

God can let a demon of hard times fall on you and everything your hand touch will fail. You can work all the time and never see the light in your situation. Your money will be like a bag with holes in it. Watch out when God begins to blow on your stuff, you look around and see what you once had and it's gone. Working from 9-5 and overtime and still you can't make it, you must give God what's due him. I am sure you don't want God to blow on what you have.

It is a bad thing to work and don't know where your money went, you had it but God blew on it. God said I will take what you thought you had. It is a demon when you stay broke all the time, the spirit of robbery is following you.

All the Money Belong to God

"The silver is mine, and the gold is mine, saith the LORD of hosts." Haggi 2:8

"The earth is the LORD's, and the fulness thereof; the world, and they that dwell therein." Psalms 24:1

Saints are funny people; I know they don't want to talk about gold. In the world you need some gold and silver. While the world is talking shortage the saints are saying that I am blessed. Everything in this world belongs to God and he has the say so and the last word in everything. If you are a saint then you need to talk the language of deliverance. Listen to me today, your words hold power.

The whole world is in a crisis and they don't have the answers. We cannot speak or say what the world or the sinners are saying, death and life is in the power of the tongue. Gas is sky high and going up all the time, I want you to know that God will provide gold and silver so you can buy all the gas you need. Don't ride up to the gas pump talking doubt and unbelief, because while you are pumping the gas God can work a miracle in your tank.

David said that the righteous will not be forsaken or his seed begging for bread. (Psalms 37:25) You must stand on your confession of the word of God. Today I speak prophetically that God can let you find a gold mine which means a person with favor on them to bless you with your need. God wants to load you down with silver and gold, for gold is money. God will draw a line between his people and the unsaved. The scripture says, *"And I will put a division between my people and thy people: tomorrow shall this sign be."Exodus 8:23*

- *"Else, if thou wilt not let my people go, behold, I will send swarms of flies upon thee, and upon thy servants, and upon thy people, and into thy houses: and the houses of the Egyptians shall be full of swarms of flies, and also the ground whereon they are. And I will sever in that day the land of Goshen, in which my people dwell, that no swarms of flies shall be there; to the end thou mayest know that I am the LORD in the midst of the earth." Exodus 8:21-22*

- *"And the LORD did that thing on the morrow, and all the cattle of Egypt died: but of the cattle of the children of Israel died not one." Exodus 9:6*

- *"Only in the land of Goshen, where the children of Israel were, was there no hail." Exodus 9:26*

- *"They saw not one another, neither rose any from his place for three days: but all the children of Israel had light in their dwellings."Exodus 10:23*

God will satisfy you during financial famine. *"The LORD knoweth the days of the upright: and their inheritance shall be for ever. They shall not be ashamed in the evil time: and in the days of famine they shall be satisfied." Psalms 37:18-19*

God Wants You to Profit

"Thus saith the LORD, thy Redeemer, the Holy One of Israel; I am the LORD thy God which teacheth thee to profit, which leadeth thee by the way that thou shouldest go." Isaiah 48:17

"I will instruct thee and teach thee in the way which thou shalt go: I will guide thee with mine eye.

Be ye not as the horse, or as the mule, which have no understanding: whose mouth must be held in with bit and bridle, lest they come near unto thee." Psalms 32:8-9

God wants to show you how you can have more than enough. God is saying I want to lead you and show you where the money is. God wants you to gain and he wants to increase you with more of his blessing. God wants to show you where your money is and whose hand your money is in.

God is placing an anointing on you to profit; God wants to show the world how he has blessed you since you received him.

2

Until Debt Do Us Part

"Now there cried a certain woman of the wives of the sons of the prophets unto Elisha, saying, Thy servant my husband is dead; and thou knowest that thy servant did fear the LORD: and the creditor is come to take unto him my two sons to be bondmen. Then she came and told the man of God. And he said, Go, sell the oil, and pay thy debt, and live thou and thy children of the rest." 2 Kings 4:1, 7

In the marriage vow it says until death do us part. It is saying we will stay together until one of us dies, until death do us part. There are so many people bound by debt and don't see no way out. There is a way that debt can depart, have faith for God to send a money anointing in your life. God want you out of debt and able to pay for what you get.

You don't want to live all your life with debt hanging over your head. People will stay together as long as things are going well. You need to layaway things when you don't have the money to pay.

Don't settle for having debts all of your life. Look for your money condition to get better.

Debts Up To My Neck

"And it shall come to pass in that day, that his burden shall be taken away from off thy shoulder, and his yoke from off thy neck, and the yoke shall be destroyed because of the anointing." Isaiah 10:27

"Though he heap up silver as the dust, and prepare raiment as the clay; He may prepare it, but the just shall put it on, and the innocent shall divide the silver." Job 27:16-17

It's time to break and destroy the debts from around your neck. It will take a supernatural anointing to do it. When you are up to your neck in debts it is hard to breathe so to speak. Debt is a spirit and we get carried away with it, it feels good at the time but when the bills begin to roll in that's when the trouble begins.

God has released his financial anointing (take it). People that are saved see no way out; it will take the anointing to get you out. It is bad to be yoked up with debts so that you can't even sleep. We need to destroy that yoke with the anointing. Your spirit is crying inside of you saying get me out of all this debt.

God is sending an end-time anointing to be released in the saints debts. You must receive this anointing in your spirit to come out of debt. You can't borrow your way out of debt; God will do it supernaturally with a divine intervention. One thing you must understand is that God will use me in prophecy and the prophetic to get you out of your money trouble, believe the prophet, *"believe his prophets, so shall ye prosper." 2 Chronicles 20:20*

Faith in God will pull you through and pull you out

of debt. Say, **"For me the anointing is on me and I wear it well."** Command the demon of debt to be rebuked off of your life right now. We must declare war on this debt demon and pay cash for what we buy. If you can't pay for it wait until you get the money.

Join the Debt Free Army. We are choking up to our neck in debt; listen to what the Holy Ghost is saying through the anointing to you. Break that yoke from around your neck. When you are up to your neck in debt it means that there is no way out. But our God is able to destroy that yoke with the anointing. The anointing will break and destroy that yoke when the prophet is packing an anointing to get you out of debt. God will send a debt cancelling anointing. It will take money or cash to buy corn beef hash.

In Debt Over Your Head

"Jesus Christ the same yesterday, and to day, and forever." Hebrews 13:8

"Ah Lord GOD! behold, thou hast made the heaven and the earth by thy great power and stretched out arm, and there is nothing too hard for thee:" Jeremiah 32:17

"For with God nothing shall be impossible." Luke 1:37

Debts on top of debts and bills on top of bills, when you look around you don't see any way out; God got a way out for you according to his word. We must learn how to trust God and take him at his word. God is still doing the impossible. You must want to be debt free and do your part to help yourself. There are things that you must do and one of them is learn how to pay cash or just wait until you have the money to get it.

There are people in the bible that had debt but God gave them a debt cancellation and paid their bills off. There are three things you must know:

1. God is a debt cancelling God.
2. God is no respecter of person.
3. God wants you to be debt free.

The bible tells the story of **a widow whose debt was cancelled,** so it goes; *"Now there cried a certain woman of the wives of the sons of the prophets unto Elisha, saying, Thy servant my husband is dead; and thou knowest that thy servant did fear the LORD: and the creditor is come to take unto him my two sons to be bondmen. And Elisha said unto her, What shall I do for thee? tell me, what hast thou in the house? And she said, Thine handmaid hath not any thing in the house, save a pot of oil. Then he said, Go, borrow thee vessels abroad of all thy neighbours, even empty vessels; borrow not a few. And when thou art come in, thou shalt shut the door upon thee and upon thy sons, and shalt pour out into all those vessels, and thou shalt set aside that which is full. So she went from him, and shut the door upon her and upon her sons, who brought the vessels to her; and she poured out. And it came to pass,* when the vessels were full, that she said unto her son, Bring me yet a vessel. And he said unto her, There is not a vessel more. And the oil stayed. Then she came and told the man of God. And he said, Go, sell the oil, and pay thy debt, and live thou and thy children of the rest." 2 Kings 4:1-7

A Nation that Became Debt Free

"And there was a great cry of the people and of their wives against their brethren the Jews. For there were that said, We, our sons, and our daughters, are many: therefore we take up corn for them, that we may eat, and live. Some also there were that said, We have mortgaged our lands, vineyards, and houses, that we might buy corn, because of the dearth. There were also that said, We have borrowed money for the king's tribute, and that upon our lands and vineyards. Yet now our flesh is as the flesh of our brethren, our children as their children: and, lo, we bring into bondage our sons and our daughters to be servants, and some of our daughters are brought unto bondage already: neither is it in our power to redeem them; for other men have our lands and vineyards. And I was very angry when I heard their cry and these words.

Then I consulted with myself, and I rebuked the nobles, and the rulers, and said unto them, Ye exact usury, every one of his brother. And I set a great assembly against them. And I said unto them, We after our ability have redeemed our brethren the Jews, which were sold unto the heathen; and will ye even sell your brethren? or shall they be sold unto us? Then held they their peace, and found nothing to answer. Also I said, It is not good that ye do: ought ye not to walk in the fear of our God because of the reproach of the heathen our enemies? I likewise, and my brethren, and my servants, might exact of them money and corn: I pray you, let us leave off this usury. Restore, I pray you, to them, even this day, their lands, their vineyards, their oliveyards, and their houses, also the hundredth part of the money, and of the corn, the wine, and the oil, that ye exact of them. Then said they, We will restore them, and will require nothing of them; so will we do as thou sayest. Then I called the priests, and took an oath of them, that they should do according to this promise." Nehemiah 5:1-12

Jesus Had a Debt Cancellation

"And when they were come to Capernaum, they that received tribute money came to Peter, and said, Doth not your master pay tribute? He saith, Yes. And when he was come into the house, Jesus prevented him, saying, What thinkest thou, Simon? of whom do the kings of the earth take custom or tribute? of their own children, or of strangers? Peter saith unto him, Of strangers. Jesus saith unto him, Then are the children free. Notwithstanding, lest we should offend them, go thou to the sea, and cast an hook, and take up the fish that first cometh up; and when thou hast opened his mouth, thou shalt find a piece of money: that take, and give unto them for me and thee." Matthew 17:24-27

My God really is a debt cancelling God.

- **Stop using Credit Cards and begin to perform plastic surgery on them.**
- **Stop impulse buying.**
- **Stop going into debt.**

Begin to speak out of your mouth **"I Am Out of Debt."** You can remove that mountain of debt, in the book of Mark 11:23 it says, *"For verily I say unto you, That whosoever shall say unto this mountain, Be thou removed, and be thou cast into the sea; and shall not doubt in his heart, but shall believe that those things which he saith shall come to pass; he shall have whatsoever he saith." Mark 11:23*

Instead of keeping up with the Jones' why don't you keep up with Jesus. Call on God and he will help you, the scripture says, *"And call upon me in the day of trouble: I will deliver thee, and thou shalt glorify me." Psalms 50:15*

God wants to put money in your path to pay off your debts. Declare that you are going debt free this year. The money anointing shall break out for you and you will be able to pay as you go. You were meant to be the head and not the tail. Free yourself from debt and paycheck to paycheck living. Trust God today and see won't he make a way for you.

Telling Debts Bye, Bye

"Then she came and told the man of God. And he said, Go, sell the oil, and pay thy debt, and live thou and thy children of the rest." 2 Kings 4:7

God wants to bring you out of debt so you can tell debt bye, bye. Debt no more is what you should be saying. Debts are demons and they keep you bound down. Sometimes you feel like there is no way out of your debts, but there is a way and God will send the anointing for debt cancellation. Some of you are up to your neck in debt, but God want to erase your debt. God wants to lift you out of that pit of debts.

You can't say bye, bye to debt and always buying on credit, how can you go debt free and always buying things on credit. We need to believe God for the whole package and trust him to give us money to take care of things in life. I want you to know that God want you to have an abundant life. God want to keep your head above the waters of debts. We want God to help us so that debt can die. What do you mean when debt die, every time you pay out a bill that ends it, that debt is dead?

When we begin to say bye, bye to debt then we need to ask God to give us a money flow. God can get you out of debt, just like he saved your soul by faith; faith in God will get you what you want. Always speak bye, bye to negative talking and thinking because you are what you confess and speak.

When you declare debt free living then that's when God will send miracle money and blessing from unknown sources. God is calling for a tax free day in your life. That means when you buy things you will not worry about the tax you will pay for God is more than enough. God wants to erase your debts and bring about a debt cancellation. You are in your miracle season, rebuke the demon of debt.

God wants to impregnate you with a spirit of debt cancellation and turn your gloom into glory. Keep sowing for your deliverance, give what you've never given before-$200, $300, $400, $500, $600, $700, you need to learn how to stretch your faith.

Saints want something for nothing, do something you've never done before and get something you've never had before.

3

Money Don't Live Here Anymore

"Ye looked for much, and, lo it came to little; and when ye brought it home, I did blow upon it. Why? saith the LORD *of hosts. Because of mine house that is waste, and ye run every man unto his own house." Haggai 1:9*

"The blessing of the LORD, *it maketh rich, and he addeth no sorrow with it." Proverbs 10:22*

Money has taken a vacation from your house, money don't live here anymore. It left your house when you fail to believe God for money. God wants you blessed, some time you may go and try to find a person that live at an address that you were told and you found out that they have moved.

Well, money will leave your house when you don't know how to handle money. Money will walk out on you and leave you holding the bag. Unpaid bills will cause money to walk out on you and make you lose what you had. **Money doesn't live here anymore.**

Money abandoned you and walked out on you, money went across town to somebody else house that could handle it. **Money doesn't live here anymore.**

Money is like a married man that will walk out on his wife. The reason money left your house is because you don't know how to handle your money. **Lord**

teach me how to be a money handler. Sometimes women will tell other women that Henry walked out on me, well when you fail to pay your tithes, money will walk out on you and leave your house and all you will be able to say is, **money doesn't live here anymore.**

Insufficient Funds

"Not that we are sufficient of ourselves to think any thing as of ourselves; but our sufficiency is of God." 2 Corinthians 3:5

"The LORD is my shepherd; I shall not want." Psalms 23:1

Sometimes you will get a return check back saying insufficient funds, meaning that you don't have enough money in the bank to cover the check. God is more than enough and he wants you to have an overflow of money in your bank account. God want you to have seed to sow, therefore you need faith for an overflow of money. God has placed an anointing on you that money will be attracted to you. In Psalms 23 it says, *"The LORD is my shepherd; I shall not want. He maketh me to lie down in green pastures: he leadeth me beside the still waters. He restoreth my soul: he leadeth me in the paths of righteousness for his name's sake. Yea, though I walk through the valley of the shadow of death, I will fear no evil: for thou art with me; thy rod and thy staff they comfort me. Thou preparest a table before me in the presence of mine enemies: thou anointest my head with oil; my cup runneth over. Surely goodness and mercy shall follow me all the days of my life: and I will dwell in the house of the LORD for ever."*

You may not write a check to someone and it bounce but you can be low in your money matters. The word of God teaches us that if we bless somebody we will reap a harvest. The bank of heaven is not broke or going broke. You can draw blessings from God that will supply your every need. There is no lack or slack in God, the Lord is your shepherd and there is no want in him.

Increase is running you down looking to give to you. God wants to pour out more than enough into your life; in this supernatural hour that we're in God will intervene on your behalf to give you more than enough. The Lord knows what you have need of before you ask and it is the will of God that you have money to pay every bill and then some left over.

Pay it Off

"Owe no man any thing, but to love one another: for he that loveth another hath fulfilled the law." Romans 13:8

"The rich ruleth over the poor, and the borrower is servant to the lender." Proverbs 22:7

Debt is a thief, I hear so many people talking about going debt free, but I want you to know how can you be debt free when you still buying stuff on credit. Debt is a demon and it possesses you and controls you until you can't help yourself. To get out of debt you must pay for what you already have. You can't borrow your way out of debt, for what you borrow you must pay the lender back. God wants you out of debt, there are people up to their necks in debt and they don't see any way out.

But if you will only trust God to pay off what you have and make God a vow that you will pay for what you buy. If you don't have the money to buy things then save until you are able to buy it cash. One thing about debt is that it will rob you out of sleep and peace of mind. When you owe everybody you will always be trying to find a way to pay them back.

A lot of people rob Peter to pay Paul, but you still owe Peter. So what you have to do is pay Peter off and then pay Paul what you owe him. God will help you get out of debt; he will teach you how to seed into your debt by paying a little here and a little there until it is paid off. You don't want to live your life under the heavy burden of debt.

People are working hard to pay off bills and come out of debt, but you must trust God to get you out. When he gets you out then you're out and you don't owe man anything.

4

A Financial Anointing

"Be not deceived; God is not mocked: for whatsoever a man soweth, that shall he also reap. For he that soweth to his flesh shall of the flesh reap corruption; but he that soweth to the Spirit shall of the Spirit reap life everlasting. And let us not be weary in well doing: for in due season we shall reap, if we faint not." Galatians 6:7-9

It is important that you sit under a leader that teaches with an anointing about money or finances. If we are to reap a money harvest we must sow seeds. Saints are looking for increase in their money but they never sow money. Give your money an assignment by naming what you want God to do for you in return for your seed.

Plant a specific seed for a specific need. You should live with expectation.

- Expectation is the powerful current that makes the seed work for you. *"But without faith it is impossible to please him: for he that cometh to God must believe that he is, and that he is a rewarder of them that diligently seek him." Hebrews 11:6*

- Expect protection as he promised. *"And I will rebuke the devourer for your sakes, and he shall not destroy the fruits of your ground; neither shall your vine cast her fruit before the time in the field, saith the LORD of hosts." Malachi 3:11*

- Expect favor from a Boaz close to you. *"Give, and it shall be given unto you; good measure, pressed down, and shaken together, and running over, shall men give into your bosom. For with the same measure that ye mete withal it shall be measured to you again." Luke 6:38*

- Expect financial ideas and wisdom from God as a harvest. *"But thou shalt remember the LORD thy God: for it is he that giveth thee power to get wealth, that he may establish his covenant which he sware unto thy fathers, as it is this day." Deuteronomy 8:18*

- Expect your enemies to fragment and be confused and flee before you. *"The LORD shall cause thine enemies that rise up against thee to be smitten before thy face: they shall come out against thee one way, and flee before thee seven ways." Deuteronomy 28:7*

- Expect God to bless you for every act of obedience. *"And it shall come to pass, if thou shalt hearken diligently unto the voice of the Lord thy*

God, to observe and to do all his commandments which I command thee this day, that the LORD thy God will set thee on high above all nations of the earth: And all these blessings shall come on thee, and overtake thee, if thou shalt hearken unto the voice of the LORD thy God." Deuteronomy 28:1-2

Reach up and grab what you're expecting and pull it down. People are not experiencing increase because no one has told them about the principle of seed faith. The unlearned are simply the untaught, teachers are necessary therefore you must sit at the feet of a teacher to learn. Everyone understand sowing and how to sow for a harvest.

- Seed faith is sowing a specific seed in faith that it will grow.
- Seed faith is letting go of something you have been given to create something else you have been promised.

Your seed is what blesses someone else, give your seed an assignment and it will bless the place where it is sown and will come back multiplied and bless you also.

Hanging With Somebody That Has A Money Anointing On Them

"And Abram went up out of Egypt, he, and his wife, and all that he had, and Lot with him, into the south. And Abram was very rich in cattle, in silver, and in gold. And

he went on his journeys from the south even to Bethel, unto the place where his tent had been at the beginning, between Bethel and Hai; Unto the place of the altar, which he had make there at the first: and there Abram called on the name of the LORD. And Lot also, which went with Abram, had flocks, and herds, and tents. And the land was not able to bear them, that they might dwell together: for their substance was great, so that they could not dwell together.

And there was a strife between the herdmen of Abram's cattle and the herdmen of Lot's cattle: and the Canaanite and the Perizzite dwelled then in the land. And Abram said unto Lot, Let there be no strife, I pray thee, between me and thee, and between my herdmen and thy herdmen; for we be brethren. Is not the whole land before thee? separate thyself, I pray thee, from me: if thou wilt take the left hand, then I will go to the right; or if thou depart to the right hand, then I will go to the left. And Lot lifted up his eyes, and beheld all the plain of Jordan, that it was well watered every where, before the LORD destroyed Sodom and Gomorrah, even as the garden of the LORD, like the land of Egypt, as thou comest unto Zoar. Then Lot chose him all the plain of Jordan; and Lot journeyed east: and they separated themselves the one from the other.

Abram dwelled in the land of Canaan, and Lot dwelled in the cities of the plain, and pitched his tent toward Sodom. But the men of Sodom were wicked and sinners before the LORD exceedingly. And the LORD said unto Abram, after that Lot was separated from him, Lift up now thine eyes, and look from the place where thou art northward, and southward, and eastward, and westward: For all the land which thou seest, to thee will I give it, and to thy seed for ever. And I will make thy seed as the dust of the earth: so that if a man can number the dust of the earth, then shall thy seed also be numbered. Arise, walk through the land in the length of it and in the breadth of it; for I will give it unto thee. Then Abram removed his tent, and came and dwelt in the plain of Mamre, which is in Hebron, and built there an altar unto the LORD." Genesis 1:18

How can two broke people help each other with no money between the two of them? How can two walk together unless they agree? Nothing from nothing leaves nothing, it is a spirit when you are broke all the time. Sometime you see people hanging with each other in close proximity, but you don't see them with nothing that looks like a blessing. When you see two winos hanging together they are looking for some wine or trying to get some money to buy some wine.

It is time for the saints to hang with somebody that got some money. You need some friends that got some money. The Lord promised Abraham and blessed him with wealth and Lot received the same blessing because he followed Abraham, that anointing rolled off on him.

As a believer you need to hang with people that have some money, people that has money anointing on them. Hang with somebody that can take you to the next level. Hang with the prophet that's packing a money anointing on him. If you are going to hang with somebody hang around blessed people that got something to offer.

Crazy people want to hang with other crazy people. If you are going to hang with somebody let it be somebody that want to have something. You need to hang with saints that are seeking to better their condition in the area of money. A money anointing is what we need to further the gospel. Hang with somebody that is prospering and trying to reach a new level in their finances and hang in there until the victory comes.

5

Giving and the Seed

"Give, and it shall be given unto you; good measure, pressed down, and shaken together, and running over, shall men give into your bosom. For with the same measure that ye mete withal it shall be measured to you again." Luke 6:38

If you give you will get, your gift will return to you in full and overflowing measure, pressed down, shaken together to make room for more and running over. Whatever measure you use to give, large or small will be used to measure what is given back to you.

Check your giving and see if what you're giving is what you want to receive. The scripture says, *"Give, and it shall be given unto you; good measure, pressed down, and shaken together, and running over, shall men give into your bosom. For with the same measure that ye mete withal it shall be measured to you again." Luke 6:38*

When you give little don't look for much. You must learn to take on the mindset of the farmer and observe their way of sowing much seed to get back an abundance of crop. When you sow little you will reap little, your measure of giving will determine the measure that you will reap. Whatever you put out will come back in the manner that you put it forth.

Individuals want to reap abundance but they're not willing to give abundantly. But in order to reap abundantly you must give in abundance. God want to send you the abundant blessing, pressed down, shaken together and running over that man will bless you real good. Become a giver and make giving a habit and your giving will open unexpected doors for you. When you give favor will rest upon you. This is your season and its harvest time for you.

When you have a running over blessing then you can bless somebody else. In this hour when people are talking about recession, as a child of God you can talk about how bless you are. Don't stop your giving, intensify your giving and watch God supercharge your finances.

Your Seed Is Anointed to Grow

"That in blessing I will bless thee, and in multiplying I will multiply thy seed as the stars of the heaven, and as the sand which is upon the sea shore; and thy seed shall possess the gate of his enemies." Genesis 22:17

I want you to know that your seed is like money in the bank, when your money is in the bank it draws interest. Your seed when given to God will grow and multiply. You may ask how my seed is anointed to grow. After you have given your seed and it has left your hands doors are open and healing takes place. Increase begins to come your way and miracle money shows up for you. When your seed is anointed to grow you begin to see the suddenly of God.

When you plant natural seed in the ground you don't go back and dig them up, you rest in the fact that you have planted the seed in good soil and you look forward to reaping a good harvest. The best time to sow a seed and watch it grow is when your money is low and that's all you have at that time. When you sow in faith during this time you are sure to reap a great harvest. A familiar story is the story about Elijah and the widow that goes like this; "*And the word of the* LORD *came unto him, saying, Arise, get thee to Zarephath, which belongeth to Zidon, and dwell there: behold, I have commanded a widow woman there to sustain thee. So he arose and went to Zarephath. And when he came to the gate of the city, behold, the widow woman was there gathering of sticks: and he called to her, and said, Fetch me, I pray thee, a little water in a vessel, that I may drink. And as she was going to fetch it, he called to her, and said, Bring me, I pray thee, a morsel of bread in thine hand. And she said, As the* LORD *thy God liveth, I have not a cake, but an handful of meal in a barrel, and a little oil in a cruse: and, behold, I am gathering two sticks, that I may go in and dress it for me and my son, that we may eat it, and die.*

And Elijah said unto her, Fear not; go and do as thou hast said: but make me thereof a little cake first, and bring it unto me, and after make for thee and for thy son. For thus saith the LORD *God of Israel, The barrel of meal shall not waste, neither shall the cruse of oil fail, until the day that the* LORD *sendeth rain upon the earth. And she went and did according to the saying of Elijah: and she, and he, and her house, did eat many days. And the barrel of meal wasted not, neither did the cruse of oil fail, according to the word of the LORD, which he spake by Elijah." 1 Kings 17:8-16*

When you give to God's work it is anointed to grow with an increase on it. When your seed leaves your hands it opens up the hand of God to move on your behalf. The Lord said he would bless the labor of your hands; therefore what you touch is anointed to grow. In the story of the two fish and five loaves we see how Jesus took this amount from the lad and blessed the people and also blessed the lad for his giving. *"When Jesus then lifted up his eyes, and saw a great company come unto him, he saith unto Philip, Whence shall we buy bread, that these may eat? And this he said to prove him: for he himself knew what he would do. Philip answered him, Two hundred pennyworth of bread is not sufficient for them, that every one of them may take a little.*

One of his disciples, Andrew, Simon Peter's brother, saith unto him, There is a lad here, which hath five barley loaves, and two small fishes: but what are they among so many? And Jesus said, Make the men sit down. Now there was much grass in the place. So the men sat down, in number about five thousand. And Jesus took the loaves; and when he had given thanks, he distributed to the disciples, and the disciples to them that were set down; and likewise of the fishes as much as they would. When they were filled, he said unto his disciples, Gather up the fragments that remain, that nothing be lost. Therefore they gathered them together, and filled twelve baskets with the fragments of the five barley loaves, which remained over and above unto them that had eaten. "John 6:5-13

You will reap what you sow, that seed faith that you plant with an expectation of a special harvest for a specific result or miracle you will see the manifestation of it according to the seed sown. And when you increase the size of your seed you automatically increased the size of your harvest. In 2 Corinthians 9:6 it says, *"But this I say, He which soweth sparingly shall reap also sparingly; and he which soweth bountifully shall reap also bountifully."*

When God talks to you about a seed he has a harvest on his mind for you. Your money is anointed to grow and when your money is anointed it will go a long way. God will stretch your money and keep you from getting down to your last dime because your money is anointed to grow.

6

Supernatural Money

"Notwithstanding, lest we should offend them, go thou to the sea, and cast an hook, and take up the fish that first cometh up; and when thou hast opened his mouth, thou shalt find a piece of money: that take, and give unto them for me and thee." Matthew 17:27

When you give you set yourself up for a miracle. When you obey God in your giving he is trying to get something to you. The more you give the more you will have. God got some miracle money coming your way, money that you have not worked for, miracle money.

In a pack of M&M's there are different colors, that is saying all kinds of money, 10, 20, 30, 40, 50, 60, 70, 80, 1000.00, 2000.00. Speak out into the atmosphere and say **"more money"**, it's not a sin to have money but the lack of money is a sin.

Don't let anybody talk you out of your blessing. Money will cause God to work great miracles in your life. Give and the more you give men will give unto you. We need miracle money, money that God will send your way from sources, peoples and places that you weren't looking for it from. God wants you to have millionaire faith and he wants to put you in a wealthy place.

A Lump Sum Miracle

"Though he heap up silver as the dust, and prepare raiment as the clay. He may prepare it, but the just shall put it on, and the innocent shall divide the silver." Job 27:16-17

" Thou preparest a table before me in the presence of mine enemies: thou anointest my head with oil; my cup runneth over." Psalms 23:5

A Lump Sum is an amount of money given in a single payment or things that equate to money. I want you to know that God got a lump sum of miracle money for you. This is the time for a money release that is on the way for you, have faith for a lump sum. With God the unexpected can happen anytime, there are people in the Bible that got a lump sum from God.

Job in the Bible lost everything that he had but when God blessed him again he received a lump sum return. If you are to get a lump sum from God you must sow a seed toward your lump sum. God is ready to give you the hundred fold blessing. Mark 10:28-31

Abraham had a lump sum anointing on his life, the lump sum anointing that was on Abraham fell on lot to the point that he had so much that he had to go to another city.

I feel a lump sum anointing working its way toward you now.

The widow woman in the Bible got a lump sum when she obeyed the man of God. She cooked the last food she had for him and got a lump sum miracle meal barrel. It's time for you to get your lump sum money so that you can pay all of your bills off and have some left over. A lump sum miracle is more than enough; we are talking about a super-abundance of money.

"Believe in the Lord your God, so shall ye be established, believe his prophets so shall ye prosper." 2 Chronicles 20:20

"If ye will not believe, surely ye shall not be established." Isaiah 7:9

Miracles happen to people that are expecting them; your miracle is on the way.

- Settlements
- Unexpected money
- Checks
- Refunds of all kinds
- Miracle money that you did not work for

- Hidden money
- Money only for your eyes

If you will stay under the anointing where the word of God is being preached you will flourish in the house of God. Through this book God is sending you a prophetic word to bring you to the next level to your miracle. This is a move of God to intervene and intercede on your behalf; you are just one step from your miracle.

Bills Caught Up Supernaturally

"The earth is the LORD's, *and the fulness thereof; the world, and they that dwell therein." Psalms 24:1*

"And he said, An hundred measures of oil. And he said unto him, Take thy bill, and sit down quickly, and write fifty. Then said he to another, And how much owest thou? And he said, An hundred measures of wheat. And he said unto him, Take thy bill, and write fourscore. And the lord commended the unjust steward, because he had done wisely: for the children of this world are in their generation wiser than the children of light." Luke 16:6-8

We need more than enough and we need an over

plus. When God bless you with extra money that is when you need to pay on your bills. When you get behind in paying your bills you must play catch up. God is moving in such a way that you will have extra money, I feel a supernatural release for money to pay out your bills. God wants your head above sinking water and it's going to take a divine intervention to do it.

Seed into your bills and pay them off. Ask God to give you money to pay off your bills. List your bills down on a sheet of paper and watch God pay them off and every time you pay one off check it off the list. There is an anointing on this word for your bills; it's time to pay all of them off. Speak out of your mouth **(My bills are paid off)**. I see bills coming down in the spirit.

Bills are holding down people to the point that they hate to even answer the telephone. Money comes to you to pay these bills off. Handle your money because God wants to bring you out from under the lender and make you the lender.

My Supernatural Source

"But my God shall supply all your need according to his

riches in glory by Christ Jesus." Philippians 4:19,

"Be not ye therefore like unto them: for your Father knoweth what things ye have need of, before ye ask him." Matthew 6:8

"The LORD is my shepherd; I shall not want." Psalms 23:1

"Commit thy way unto the LORD; trust also in him; and he shall bring it to pass." Psalms 37:25

Definition for Source: Any person, place or thing by which something is supplied.

Your job is not your source but God is your source, we look to the wrong peoples and the wrong things for our help. Your help is in the name of the Lord.

When your jobs fail and the boss tell you they will be a lay-off, we say to each other what am I going to do the answer is to trust God. I want you to rest assured that the Lord is your shepherd and you shall not want. You must look to the hills from whence come your help.

You must begin to say to yourself—**Help is on the way**! David said, "I have never seen the righteous forsaken or his seed begging for bread." (Psalms 37:25) One thing about God is he will take care of his own. God is a present help in the time of trouble.

When your back is up against the wall and it looks like there is no way out, Jesus can bring you up and out of any troubles. The Lord will supply your every need, the world and everything in it belongs to God.

Lift up your hands and say, *"All my needs are met and all my bills are paid."*

A lot of jobs are laying off and people are wondering what to do. You must put your total trust in the Lord to see you through. God is your supernatural provider:

- Your money provider
- Your bill payer
- Your house mortgage or rent provider
- Your car note maker
- Your light bill man
- Your bread and meat provider
- What he can't do just can't be done

Trust my Lord today and see doesn't he make a way

because he is a way maker. We must learn to get off the **world system** and get on the **word system**. If you are a child of God you will be provided for by your heavenly Father. All of your needs are met and God will not let you go under before he will let you go over. One thing about God is that he is our helper.

- *"Thou hast seen it; for thou beholdest mischief and spite, to requite it with thy hand: the poor committeth himself unto thee; thou art the helper of the fatherless." Psalms 10:14*

- *"Hear, O LORD, and have mercy upon me: LORD, be thou my helper." Psalms 30:10*

- *"For he shall deliver the needy when he crieth; the poor also, and him that hath no helper." Psalms 72:12*

- *"So that we may boldly say, The Lord is my helper, and I will not fear what man shall do unto me." Hebrews 13:6*

Help Is On the Way

7

Money Begets Money

"Wealth maketh many friends; but the poor is separated from his neighbour." Proverbs 19:4

I hear money calling your name, money is looking for you. Money draws money and God want to make you a money magnet. The more you give it comes back to you in double abundance. The anointing will cause money to come your way, God will move on somebody supernaturally to give you some money. Let me hear you say, **"I Feel Money Coming."**

It's on me and I wear it well, what's on me, a money anointing. Money is on its way to your address, look for it in your mail box, miracle money is being released your way. God wants to work for you, *"It is time for thee, LORD, to work: for they have made void thy law." Psalms 119:126* If you want more money then you must watch your words, *"Thou art snared with the words of thy mouth, thou art taken with the words of thy mouth."Proverbs 6:2*

I want you to know that you will reap money when you give it, *"The desire of the righteous is only good: but the expectation of the wicked is wrath. There is that scattereth, and yet increaseth; and there is that withholdeth more than is meet, but it tendeth to poverty. The liberal soul shall be made fat: and he that watereth shall be watered also himself." Proverbs 11:23-25*

It is all right to love people but love doesn't pay any bills. You can't go to the electric company and tell them, *"I don't have the money to pay my bill this month but I love you"* or go to your phone company and tell them *"I know my bill is due this month but I don't have the money but I just want you to know that I love you all."* They will look at you like you are crazy; you must go to these companies with the m-o-n-e-y.

You must begin to stretch your faith and begin to give $50, $75, $100 and even a $1,000. It will take the anointing to get you out of your debts. God will use somebody that will show you favor. When God bless you with money there is a mission that he uses for his kingdom. The giving anointing is working in you and when you sow expect a great harvest. Money with a mission to send the gospel throughout the whole earth so that souls can be saved set free and delivered.

Money Words Definitions

- Miracle Money = M&M
- Have Money to Burn = to have more money than one needs, so that some can be spent foolishly. Proverbs 19:4

- In the Money = among the winners as in a contest, to be prosperous, wealthy and successful. Deuteronomy 8:18

- Make Money = to gain profits, become wealthy. Isaiah 48:17, Psalms 32:8

- On the Money = exact, correct. The prediction was right on the money.

- Money Magnet = *"The LORD shall increase you more and more, you and your children."* Psalms 115:14

- Money Coming to Me = *"I will lift up mine eyes unto the hills, from whence cometh my help."* Psalms 121:1

- Stand on Your Money Confession = keep speaking the word over your situations until you see it manifest.

Miracle money is money that you did not work for. You must speak the word of deliverance in order to see the supernatural manifestations of God in your life. Speak the word that will bring about a change in your financial life—**Money Cometh to Me!**

- Money is looking for you.
- Millions and millions dollars.
- God doesn't want you broke, he wants you blessed.

Just like there was money in the fish mouth, the miracle is in your mouth, you must call those things that be not as though they were. You got to think miracles, think money and stay positive.

On one occasion Jesus needed some money to pay a bill, the taxes needed to be paid, so Jesus told Peter to go fishing and when he caught the first fish there would be money in his mouth to pay the taxes (Hallelujah). You must speak to money and put a demand on it, begin to speak things as though they were. **"I Feel Money Coming."**

Money wants to answer some of your prayers and desires, the scripture says, *"A feast is made for laughter, and wine maketh merry: but money answereth all things." Ecclesiastes 10:19* If you are a child of God there is an anointing on you for money, lift your hands and say **"Money is coming to these hands."**

Your breakthrough for more money is upon you right now. The devil has made many of the saints feel like it was wrong to have money. God wants you to live a blessed life and have the things you desire. God is fed up with you advertising his kingdom broke, money draws money and God wants to raise you from the dunghill.

Money talk and broke folks walk. Money is getting ready to knock on your door. Money is ready to pay off all your bills. Speak into the atmosphere right now and say, **"Money I hear you knocking, so come on in."** Money is saying I found the right person at the right address and I'm here to give you abundance, I want to bring wealth and riches in your house. *"And they rose early in the morning, and went forth into the wilderness of Tekoa: and as they went forth, Jehoshaphat stood and said, Hear me, O Judah, and ye inhabitants of Jerusalem; Believe in the* LORD *your God, so shall ye be established; believe his prophets, so shall ye prosper."* 2 Chronicles 20:20

THERE IS A MONEY ANOINTING ON YOU NOW, RECEIVE IT!

Made in the USA
Columbia, SC
15 November 2024

46498965R00033